Classic Recipes of
MEXICO

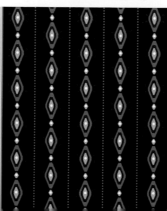

Classic Recipes of
MEXICO

TRADITIONAL FOOD AND COOKING
IN 25 AUTHENTIC DISHES

JANE MILTON

LORENZ BOOKS

This edition is published by
Lorenz Books,
an imprint of Anness Publishing Ltd,
108 Great Russell Street,
London WC1B 3NA
info@anness.com
www.annesspublishing.com
twitter: @Anness_Books

If you like the images in this book and
would like to investigate using them for
publishing, promotions or advertising,
please visit our website
www.practicalpictures.com for more
information.

Publisher: Joanna Lorenz
Editor: Helen Sudell
Designer: Nigel Partridge
Recipe Photography: Simon Smith
Food Stylist: Caroline Barty
Production Controller: Rosanna Anness

A CIP catalogue record for this book is
available from the British Library

PUBLISHER'S NOTE

PUBLISHER'S ACKNOWLEDGMENTS

The Publisher would like to thank the
following agencies for the use of their
images. Istock p4, 5, 6, 8 (top) 9, 10 (top)
11 (both), 13.

Previously published as part of a larger
volume *The Food and Cooking of Mexico*.

COOK'S NOTES

Bracketed terms are intended for American
readers. For all recipes, quantities are given
in both metric and imperial measures and,
where appropriate, in standard cups and
spoons. Follow one set of measures, but
not a mixture, because they are not
interchangeable.

Standard spoon and cup measures are
level. 1 tsp = 5ml, 1 tbsp = 15ml, 1 cup =
250ml/8fl oz. Australian standard
tablespoons are 20ml. Australian readers
should use 3 tsp in place of 1 tbsp for
measuring small quantities.

American pints are 16fl oz/2 cups.
American readers should use 20fl oz/2.5
cups in place of 1 pint when measuring
liquids.

Electric oven temperatures in this book are
for conventional ovens. When using a fan
oven, the temperature will probably need to
be reduced by about 10–20ºC/20–40ºF.
Since ovens vary, you should check with
your manufacturer's instruction book for
guidance.

The nutritional analysis given for each
recipe is calculated per portion (i.e. serving
or item), unless otherwise stated. If the
recipe gives a range, such as Serves 4–6,
then the nutritional analysis will be for the
smaller portion size, i.e. 6 servings. The
analysis does not include optional
ingredients, such as salt added to taste.

Medium (US large) eggs are used unless
otherwise stated.

Contents

Introduction

Mexican food mirrors the culture of the country – it is vibrant, rich, stimulating and festive. From the wild and barren north to the sultry heat of the south, this vast country offers the food lover a feast of flavours. The waters of the Gulf of Mexico and the Pacific Ocean teem with fish, while the sub-tropical regions that adjoin them yield abundant fruit, including pineapples and papayas. Chillies of every shape, colour and size are everywhere, their taste ranging from subtle to strident, providing the signature to one of the world's most exciting cuisines.

Left: Colourful fishing boats line the shore at Cancun on the Yucatan peninsula.

Mexican Food and Cooking

Many traditional Mexican dishes are labour-intensive, reflecting the old society where the women worked all day long collecting the food required and then preparing it. Even today, the traditional meal patterns are still observed, especially in rural areas, with the main meal being eaten at midday.

Eating traditions

The day begins with *desayuno*, a light meal of coffee and a bread or pastry. By 11 am most Mexicans are ready for a more substantial dish. *Almuerzo* is

Below: Pastries are eaten daily by many Mexicans.

Above: Street vendors selling tortillas, filled with spicy meat or vegetables, are very popular.

more brunch than breakfast, and usually includes an egg dish such as *Huevos Rancheros*, with corn tortillas and plenty of coffee or fruit juice.

Comida is the main meal of the day, generally eaten about 3pm. Made up of several courses, soup is almost always served followed by a rice or pasta dish. The aptly named *platillo fuerte* (heavy dish) is the main attraction, consisting of a meat or fish stew accompanied with tortillas, salad and refried beans. The meal closes with *postre* (dessert) and an after-dinner coffee. The day ends with *merienda*, a light supper, often made up of cold leftovers from the comida.

Snack foods

Mexicans love to snack. Street food is very popular and stalls equipped with steamers sell *tamales* – little corn husk parcels filled with fiery spiced meat or cheese – from first thing in the morning, so that shift workers can still have the almuerzo even if they cannot get home. Later in the day, the stalls sell corn soup or *menudo*, a soup made with tripe and served with tortillas. In the evening the stalls sell *quesadillas*, *enchiladas* and *antojitos* (little fried nibbles). On the coast, traders sell prawns (shrimp) grilled on skewers, *ceviche* (marinated raw fish) threaded on sticks, or *elotes* – tender cobs of cooked corn dipped in cream and sprinkled with well-flavoured crumbly cheese and lime juice.

Right: Elotes are a much-loved street snack.

Mexican Festivals

Long before Christianity came to Mexico, the Indians worshipped gods whom they believed provided their food. Feast days, when people brought specific foods as offerings to the gods, were frequent events. When Christianity spread through Mexico many of these days were appropriated by the Church and either assigned as saints' days or linked to celebrations marking important days in the religious calendar.

Below: King's Day Bread takes centre stage at Christmas.

January 6
Dia de los Santos Reyes
As the culmination of two weeks of Christmas festivities, January 6th marks the meeting between the Magi – the Three Kings – and the infant Jesus. Mexicans commemorate that historical exchange of gifts with ceremonies of their own, and this is the day on which Christmas presents are given and received between family members. Central to the celebration is the King's Day Bread, a yeasted sweet bread ring filled with crystallized fruit, covered with drizzled icing and decorated with plenty of candied fruit jewels.

Carnival
The weekend before the start of Lent sees the beginning of a five-day carnival, a final joyous fling before the six-week period of self-denial. Processions of brightly coloured floats, dancing in the street and a large amount of feasting and drinking are all characteristic of this popular Christian celebration.

Above: There is much dancing in the street during Carnival.

Semana Santa
Holy week – the period leading up to Easter Day – is an important time in the Mexican calendar, notably for the many Catholics in the country. One custom is the breaking of confetti-filled eggs over the heads of friends and family.

Independence Day
A holiday to mark the day (16 September) in 1810 when the revolt against Spanish rule

began. Outside Mexico, the festival is often promoted in local Mexican restaurants and bars.

Los dias de los muertes

Commonly called The Day of the Dead, this is in fact a two-day festival, that combines in one both the ancient Aztec tradition of worship of the dead and the Christian festival of All Saints' Day on 1st November.

The festival originally came about because of a widely held

Below: Decorated graves on the Day of the Dead.

belief that the souls of the dead are permitted to spend a brief period on earth every year – like a holiday – to give their families a chance to spend time with them. Family members gather at the graveside, bringing the favourite foods of the deceased person, as well as other symbolic dishes that are traditionally eaten on this day. The foods include a pumpkin dessert and tamales. Although the festival celebrates the dead it is seen as a joyous occasion.

Navidad – Christmas Day

For 12 days before Christmas Day, the festival is heralded by processions – called *posadas* – depicting Joseph, with Mary on the donkey, searching for a room at the inn. Christmas Day sees the start of a two-week family holiday for most Mexicans. On the afternoon of the day itself families share a special meal. This traditionally starts with the sharing of the *rosca* – a sweet ring-shaped loaf with a small ceramic doll representing the infant Jesus

Above: Tamales feature in most Mexican festival celebrations.

baked inside it. Whoever finds the doll in their slice of cake must host a party on February 2nd, *Día de Candelaria* (Candlemas). The high point of the Christmas feast is the main course, when *mole poblano*, a rich turkey dish made with chillies, nuts, tomatoes, garlic, cinnamon and chocolate is served. It is accompanied by *tamales blancos* – corn husk parcels filled with a mixture that is based on white cornmeal.

Classic Ingredients

Mexico is blessed with an abundance of fresh ingredients, most of which are now readily available outside of Mexico.

Corn

The native Indians of Mexico regarded corn as a gift from the gods as it was such a hardy and adaptable food, able to flourish in so many different climates and soil types. Every part of the corn cob is used in Mexican culture: the husks for wrapping tamales, the kernels for food and the stalks for animal feed. Corn flour, *masa harina*, is used to make corn tortillas, popular in the south of the country. In the north, wheat flour tortillas are preferred by home cooks.

Below: Mexican cooks use every part of the corn cob.

Beans and rice

Dried beans are a staple food in Mexico, and there will be a pot of beans simmering daily on the cooker top in every home. Fresh beans, such as French and runner are eaten too, but it is the dried beans, with the better keeping properties, that are most widely used. Pinto, black beans and chickpeas are the most popular varieties and appear in soups, as fillings for tortillas, in many meat dishes, and on their own in salads and salsas.

Mexicans have been using rice since it was introduced to the country by the Spanish in the 16th century. White long grain rice that has had the husk removed is most common and is used in a variety of dishes from soup to rice pudding.

Fruits

Visit any Mexican market and you will be struck by the vibrant displays of fruit of every size, shape and colour. Fruit is an important part of the Mexican diet, providing the vitamins to balance the corn and beans. Citrus fruit grows well here and because the fruit is allowed to ripen on the trees, it tends to have a very good flavour.

Tropical fruits, such as granadillas, guavas and pineapples feature in many salads, salsas and desserts. But perhaps the most popular tropical fruit in Mexico is the mango, with its wonderful perfume when ripe. Mexicans tend to eat mangoes as they are but they also feature in desserts.

Popular all over South America, prickly pears grow wild and are served as a staple food in some of the poorer rural areas of Mexico. The fruit is valued for its pulp, which has a sweet aromatic flavour, rather like that of melons, but even more subtle. Prickly pears feature in fruit salads and can also be made into jelly or jam.

Right: Mango fruits ripening on the tree.

Above: Avocado is the main ingredient in guacamole.

Fruit vegetables

There are some fruits which are used so often in savoury dishes that we tend to think of them as vegetables. Tomatoes are the obvious example, but avocados, plantains, (bell) peppers and chillies also come into this varied category.

Avocados are used extensively in Mexican cookery, most famously in guacamole, the mashed avocado dip. They are also used in soups or to make a hot sauce for meat.

Tomatoes sold in Mexican markets will have ripened naturally, and will be full of flavour. They are used in a wide variety of recipes in Mexican cooking including hot and cold soups, salsas, salads and meat and fish dishes. Chopped tomatoes are added to beans to make *frijoles*, are mixed with avocados in guacamole and are used in the drink *sangrita*.

Plantains are a type of banana with a mild flavour similar to a squash. They are used in both sweet and savoury dishes. Fried plantain slices are delicious with a chilli dip or simply a squeeze of lime and a sprinkling of chilli powder. For a delectable dessert, cook them in butter and cinnamon, with a little sugar and a good measure of rum.

Sometimes known as bell peppers or capsicums, sweet peppers add colour and flavour to salsas, stews and meat fillings. They are normally cored, seeded and chopped for use in salads, but for cooked dishes, it is more usual for them to be roasted and skinned first.

Over 150 indigenous varieties of chillies are found in Mexico and range from very mild to searingly hot. The heat level

Above: Chillies are an inherent part of Mexican cooking.

of a chilli is determined by the amount of capsaicin it contains. This compound is concentrated mainly in the ribs and seeds so you can reduce the fieriness by removing these parts.

Vegetables

Mexico's indigenous peoples were very good agriculturists, and when the Spanish invaded they found a country blessed with abundant vegetables including corn (maize), sweet potatoes, jicama, pumpkins and courgettes (zucchini).

Green beans have been growing in the Americas for hundreds of years. In Mexico lima (fava) beans are widely used, as are French or string beans. Sweet potatoes are used in both sweet and savoury dishes, either cooked in their skins, or peeled and boiled. A sweet potato mash, with tomatoes and chillies, is a wonderful accompaniment to barbecued food.

Jicama is the root of a climbing bean plant. The moist flesh tastes slightly fruity, and the texture resembles that of a crisp green apple or a water chestnut. Raw jicama makes a refreshing snack when sprinkled with freshly squeezed orange juice and

Below: Sweet potatoes are a staple food for many Mexicans.

served with chilli powder and salt. It is also delicious added to salads and in salsa.

Chocolate

When the Spanish reached Mexico, one of their greatest finds was chocolate. The Aztecs were partial to a drink made from the beans of the cacao tree, which they flavoured in many different ways, and the Spanish, like the rest of the world after them, enthusiastically embraced this wonderful new taste.

Alcoholic drinks

Mexico has a good range of fermented beverages, mainly derived from fruit or a plant called the agave. Beer production is an important part of the economy and some Mexican beers such as Corona, Sol and Dos Equis are exported around the world. Pulque is a beer-like drink made from the sap of the agave plant, which is commonly called *maguey* in Mexico. It has a unique, slightly earthy flavour, and is definitely an acquired taste. Kahlua is a

Above: Margarita is a classic cocktail that features Tequila.

coffee liqueur made in Mexico city and is a popular cocktail ingredient all over the world.

Tequila is, without doubt, the Mexican spirit which is best known outside the country. The name means 'volcano' in the local Indian dialect. Drinking a shot of tequila, with a lick of salt beforehand and a wedge of lime after, is one of the best ways to sample this drink. A natural progression from the tequila shot is the margarita, where the rim of the glass is dipped in salt, the lime juice and tequila are combined and triple sec is added. Tequila and tomato juice create a Bloody Maria.

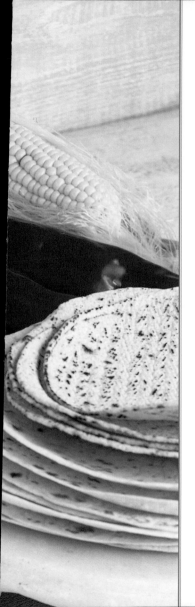

Mexican Flavours

Across the length and breadth of Mexico, the very different types of terrain and variations in climate provide a remarkable range of ingredients for the Mexican cook. Mexicans are resourceful and make good use of their native foods, as well as adapting many of the ingredients and recipes brought by successive settlers. From authentic street food such as Tacos with Shredded Beef and Quesadillas to vibrant Tomato Salsa, and from the classic Chicken Fajitas to a creamy Coconut Custard, the recipes presented here offer a lively introduction to this exciting cuisine.

Left: A tempting selection of ingredients native to Mexico.

Tomato Salsa

Serves 6 as an accompaniment
3–6 fresh serrano chillies
1 large white onion
grated rind and juice of 2 limes, plus
     strips of lime rind, to garnish
8 ripe, firm tomatoes
large bunch of coriander (cilantro)
1.5ml/¼ tsp caster (superfine) sugar
salt

*This is the traditional
tomato-based salsa that
most people associate with
Mexican food. There are
many recipes for it, but
onion, tomato, chilli and
coriander are common to
every one of them.*

1 Use three chillies for a salsa of medium heat; up to six if you like it hot. To peel the chillies spear them on a long-handled metal skewer and roast them over the flame of a gas burner until the skins blister and darken. Do not let the flesh burn. Alternatively, dry fry them on a griddle pan until the skins are scorched.

2 Place the roasted chillies in a strong plastic bag and tie the top of the bag to keep the steam in. Set aside for about 20 minutes.

3 Meanwhile, chop the onion finely and put it in a bowl with the lime rind and juice. The lime juice will soften the onion.

4 Remove the chillies from the bag and peel off the skins. Cut off the stalks, then slit the chillies and scrape out the seeds with a sharp knife. Chop the flesh roughly and set aside.

5 To remove the skins from the tomatoes, cut a small cross in the base of each tomato. Place the tomatoes in a heatproof bowl and pour over boiling water to cover.

6 Leave the tomatoes in the water for 3 minutes, then lift them out using a slotted spoon and plunge them into a bowl of cold water. Drain. The skins will have begun to peel back from the crosses. Remove the skins completely.

7 Dice the peeled tomatoes and put them in a bowl. Add the chopped onion which should have softened, together with the lime mixture. Chop the fresh coriander finely.

8 Add the coriander to the salsa, with the chillies and the sugar. Mix gently until the sugar has dissolved and all the ingredients are coated in lime juice. Season, if needed. Cover and chill for 2–3 hours to allow the flavours to blend. The salsa will keep for 3–4 days in the refrigerator. Garnish with the strips of lime rind just before serving.

Guacamole

Serves 6–8
4 medium tomatoes, skins removed
 (see page 18)
4 ripe avocados, preferably fuerte
juice of 1 lime
½ small onion
2 garlic cloves
small bunch of coriander (cilantro),
 chopped
3 fresh red fresno chillies
salt
tortilla chips, to serve

1 Cut the peeled tomatoes in half, remove the seeds with a teaspoon, then chop the flesh roughly and set it aside.

2 Cut the avocados in half then remove the stones. Scoop the flesh out of the shells and place it in a food processor or blender. Process until almost smooth, then scrape into a bowl and stir in the lime juice.

3 Chop the onion finely, then crush the garlic. Add both to the avocado and mix well. Stir in the coriander.

4 Remove the stalks from the chillies, slit them and scrape out the seeds with a small sharp knife. Chop the chillies finely and add them to the avocado mixture, with the chopped tomatoes. Mix well.

5 Check the seasoning and add salt to taste. Cover closely with clear film (plastic wrap) or a tight-fitting lid and chill for 1 hour before serving as a dip with tortilla chips. If it is well covered, guacamole will keep in the refrigerator for 2–3 days.

One of the best-loved Mexican salsas, this blend of creamy avocado, tomatoes, chillies, coriander and lime now appears on tables the world over. Bought guacamole usually contains mayonnaise, which helps to preserve the avocado, but this is not an ingredient in traditional Mexican recipes.

Black Bean Salsa

Serves 4 as an accompaniment

130g/4½ oz/generous ½ cup black
beans, soaked overnight in water
to cover
1 pasado chilli
2 fresh red fresno chillies
1 red onion
grated rind and juice of 1 lime
30ml/2 tbsp Mexican beer (optional)
15ml/1 tbsp olive oil
small bunch of coriander (cilantro),
chopped
salt

This salsa has a very striking appearance. It is rare to find a black sauce and it provides a wonderful contrast to the more common reds and greens on the plate. The pasado chillies add a subtle citrus flavour. Leave the salsa for a day or two after making to allow the flavours to develop fully.

1 Drain the beans and put them in a large pan. Pour in water to cover and place the lid on the pan. Bring to the boil, then simmer the beans for about 40 minutes or until tender. Drain, rinse under cold water, then drain again and leave the beans until cold.

2 Soak the pasado chilli in hot water for about 10 minutes until softened. Drain, remove the stalk, then slit the chilli and scrape out the seeds with a small sharp knife. Chop the flesh finely.

3 Dry fry the fresno chilies in a griddle pan until the skins are scorched. Then place the roasted chillies in a strong plastic bag and tie the top to keep the steam in. Set aside for 20 minutes.

4 Meanwhile, chop the red onion finely. Remove the chillies from the bag and peel off the skins. Slit them, remove the seeds and chop finely.

5 Tip the beans into a bowl and add the onion and both types of chilli. Stir in the lime rind and juice, beer, oil and coriander. Season with salt and mix well. Chill before serving.

Mango Salsa

Serves 4 as an accompaniment
2 fresh red fresno chillies
2 ripe mangoes
½ white onion
small bunch of coriander (cilantro)
grated rind and juice of 1 lime

This has a fresh, fruity taste and is perfect with fish or as a contrast to rich, creamy dishes. The bright colours make it an attractive addition to any table.

1 To peel the chillies spear them on a long-handled metal skewer and roast them over the flame of a gas burner until the skins blister and darken. Do not let the flesh burn. Alternatively, dry fry them in a griddle pan until the skins are scorched.

2 Place the roasted chillies in a strong plastic bag and tie the top to keep the steam in. Set aside for 20 minutes.

3 Meanwhile, put one of the mangoes on a board and cut off a thick slice close to the flat side of the stone. Turn the mango round and repeat on the other side. Score the flesh on each thick slice with criss-cross lines at 1cm/½in intervals, taking care not to cut through the skin. Repeat with the second mango.

4 Fold the mango halves inside out so that the mango flesh stands proud of the skin, in neat dice. Carefully slice these off the skin and into a bowl. Cut off the flesh adhering to each stone, dice it and add it to the bowl.

5 Remove the roasted chillies from the bag and carefully peel off the skins. Cut off the stalks, then slit the chillies and scrape out the seeds.

6 Chop the white onion and the coriander finely and add them to the diced mango. Chop the chilli flesh finely and add it to the mixture in the bowl, together with the lime rind and juice. Stir well to mix, cover and chill for at least 1 hour before serving. The salsa will keep for 2–3 days in the refrigerator.

COOK'S TIP
Mangoes, in season, are readily available nowadays, but are usually sold unripe. Keep in a warm room for 24 hours or until they are just soft to the touch. Do not allow to ripen beyond this point.

Red Rub

Makes enough for one joint of meat or four chicken breasts

10ml/2 tsp achiote (annatto) seeds
5ml/1 tsp black peppercorns
5ml/1 tsp allspice berries
5ml/1 tsp dried oregano
2.5ml/½ tsp ground cumin
5ml/1 tsp freshly squeezed lime juice
1 small Seville orange

This "rub" or dry paste is frequently used in the Yucatan for seasoning meat.

1 Put the achiote (annatto) seeds in a mortar and grind them with a pestle to a fine powder. Add the peppercorns, grind again, then repeat the process with the allspice berries. Mix in the oregano and cumin.

2 Add the lime juice to the spice mixture. Squeeze the orange and add the juice to the spice mixture a teaspoonful at a time until a thick paste is produced. Don't be tempted to substitute a sweet orange if Seville oranges are out of season; the spice mixture must be tart.

3 Allow the paste to stand for at least 30 minutes so the spices absorb the juice. The correct consistency for the paste is slightly dry and crumbly. When ready to use, rub the paste on to the surface of the meat, then leave to marinate for at least 1 hour before cooking, preferably overnight. The rub will keep for up to 1 week in a covered bowl in the refrigerator, after which time some of the flavour will be lost.

Red Salsa

Makes about 250ml/8fl oz/1 cup

3 large tomatoes
15ml/1 tbsp olive oil
3 ancho chillies and 2 pasilla chillies
2 garlic cloves, peeled and left whole
2 spring onions (scallions)
10ml/2 tsp soft dark brown sugar
2.5ml/½ tsp paprika
juice of 1 lime
2.5ml/½ tsp dried oregano
salt

Use this as a condiment with fish or meat dishes.

1 Preheat the oven to 200°C/400°F/Gas 6. Quarter the tomatoes and place in a roasting tin. Drizzle over the oil. Roast for about 40 minutes until slightly charred, then remove the skin.

2 Soak the chillies in hot water for about 10 minutes. Drain, remove the stalks, slit and then scrape out the seeds. Chop finely. Dry roast the garlic in a heavy-based pan until golden.

3 Finely chop most of the spring onions and place in a bowl with the sugar, paprika, lime juice and oregano. Slice the remaining spring onion diagonally and set aside for the garnish.

4 Put the tomatoes, chillies and garlic in a blender and process. Add the sugar, paprika, lime juice, spring onions and oregano to the blender. Process for a few seconds, then season as required. Spoon into a pan and warm through before serving garnished with the spring onion.

Chillies Rellenos

Makes 6

6 fresh poblano or Anaheim chillies
2 potatoes, total weight about
  400g/14oz
200g/7oz/scant 1 cup cream cheese
200g/7oz/1¾ cups grated mature
  (sharp) Cheddar cheese
5ml/1 tsp salt
2.5ml/½ tsp ground black pepper
2 eggs, separated
115g/4oz/1 cup plain (all-purpose)
  flour
2.5ml/½ tsp white pepper
oil, for frying
chilli flakes to garnish, optional

1 Make a neat slit down one side of each chilli. Place them in a dry frying pan over a moderate heat, turning them frequently until the skins blister.

2 Place the chillies in a strong plastic bag and tie the top. Set aside for 20 minutes, then peel off the skins and remove the seeds through the slits, keeping the chillies whole. Dry the chillies and set them aside.

3 Scrub or peel the potatoes and cut them into 1cm/½ in dice. Bring a large pan of water to the boil, add the potatoes and let the water return to boiling point. Lower the heat and simmer for 5 minutes or until the potatoes are just tender. Do not overcook. Drain them thoroughly.

4 Put the cream cheese in a bowl and stir in the grated cheese, with 2.5ml/½ tsp of the salt and the black pepper. Gently mix in the potato.

5 Spoon some of the potato filling into each chilli. Put them on a plate, cover and chill for 1 hour so that the filling becomes firm.

6 Put the egg whites in a clean, grease-free bowl and whisk them to firm peaks. In a separate bowl, beat the yolks until pale, then fold in the whites. Scrape the mixture on to a large, shallow dish. Place the flour in another dish and season it with salt and white pepper.

7 Heat the oil for deep frying to 190ºC/375ºF. Coat a few chillies first in flour and then in egg before adding carefully to the hot oil.

8 Fry the chillies in batches until golden and crisp. Drain on kitchen paper and serve hot, garnished with a sprinkle of chilli flakes for extra heat, if desired.

Stuffed chillies are popular all over Mexico. The type of chilli used differs from region to region, but larger chillies are easier to stuff than smaller ones. Poblanos and Anaheims are quite mild, but you can use hotter chillies if you prefer.

Quesadillas

Serves 4

1 fresh fresno chilli
8 wheat flour tortillas, about
   15cm/6in across
200g/7oz mozzarella, coarsely grated
Onion Relish (see cook's tip) or
   Tomato Salsa (page 18), to serve

COOK'S TIP

To make the onion relish *cebollas en escabeche*, thinly slice two white onions and 2 dry fried fresno chillies (skins removed) and place in a bowl with 5ml/1 tsp each of ground allspice berries, black peppercorns and dried oregano. Add 300ml/10fl oz/1⅓ cups white wine vinegar and stir to blend. Add salt to taste and mix thoroughly. Cover and chill for at least 1 day before use.

These cheese-filled tortillas are the Mexican equivalent of toasted sandwiches. Serve them as soon as they are cooked, or they will become chewy.

1 Spear the chilli on a long-handled metal skewer and roast it over the flame of a gas burner until the skin blisters and darkens. Alternatively, dry fry it in a griddle pan. Place the roasted chilli in a strong plastic bag and tie the top to keep the steam in. Set aside for 20 minutes.

2 Remove the chilli from the bag and carefully peel off the skin. Cut off the stalk, then slit the chilli and scrape out the seeds. Cut the flesh into eight thin strips.

3 Warm a large frying pan or griddle. Place one tortilla on the pan or griddle at a time, sprinkle about an eighth of the cheese on to one half and add a strip of chilli. Fold the tortilla over the cheese and press the edges together gently to seal. Cook the filled tortilla for 1 minute, then turn over and cook the other side for 1 minute.

4 Remove the filled tortilla from the pan or griddle, cut it into three triangles and serve at once, with the onion relish or tomato salsa.

Eggs Rancheros

Serves 4

2 corn tortillas, several days old
oil, for frying
8 eggs
1 garlic clove, crushed
4 spring onions (scallions), finely
  chopped
1 large tomato, peeled and diced
  finely (see page 18)
2 fresh green jalapeño chillies,
  roasted, peeled and chopped
  finely
150ml/¼ pint/⅔ cup single (light)
  cream
small bunch of coriander (cilantro),
  finely chopped
salt and ground black pepper

1 Cut the tortillas into long strips. Pour oil into a frying pan to a depth of 1cm/½ in. Heat the oil until it is very hot and fry the tortilla strips in batches until they are crisp and golden, then drain on kitchen paper.

2 Put the eggs in a bowl, season with salt and pepper and beat lightly.

3 Heat 15ml/1 tbsp oil in a frying pan. Add the garlic and spring onions and fry gently for 2–3 minutes until soft. Stir in the diced tomato and cook for 3–4 minutes more, then stir in the chillies and cook for 1 minute.

4 Pour the eggs into the pan and stir until they start to set. When only a small amount of uncooked egg remains visible, stir in the cream so that the cooking process is slowed down and the mixture cooks to a creamy mixture rather than a solid mass. Season to taste.

5 Stir the chopped coriander into the scrambled egg. Arrange the tortilla strips on four serving plates and spoon the eggs over. Serve at once.

There are many variations on this popular dish, which is great for breakfast or brunch. The combination of creamy eggs with onion, chilli and tomatoes works wonderfully well.

Chicken Fajitas

1 Slice the chicken breasts into 2cm/¾ in wide strips and place these in a bowl. Add the lime rind and juice, sugar, oregano, cayenne and cinnamon. Mix thoroughly. Set aside to marinate for at least 30 minutes.

2 Meanwhile, make the tortillas. Mix the flour, baking powder and salt in a large bowl. Rub in the lard, then add the warm water, a little at a time, to make a stiff dough. Knead this on a lightly floured surface for 10–15 minutes until it is smooth and elastic.

3 Divide the dough into 12 small balls, then roll each ball to a 15cm/6in round. Cover the rounds with plastic or clear film (plastic wrap) to keep them from drying out while you prepare the vegetables.

4 Cut the onions in half and slice them thinly. Cut the peppers in half, remove the cores and seeds, then slice the flesh into strips.

5 Heat a frying pan or griddle and cook each tortilla for 1 minute on each side, or until the surface colours and begins to blister. Keep the cooked tortillas warm and pliable by wrapping them in a clean, dry dish towel.

6 Heat the oil in a large frying pan. Stir-fry the marinated chicken for 5–6 minutes, then add the peppers and onions and cook for 3–4 minutes more, until the chicken strips are cooked through and the vegetables are soft and tender, but still juicy. Spoon the chicken mixture into a bowl.

7 To serve, each guest takes a warm tortilla, spreads it with a little salsa, adds a spoonful of guacamole and piles some of the chicken mixture in the centre. The final touch is to add a small dollop of sour cream. The tortilla is then folded over the filling and eaten in the hand.

Serves 6

3 skinless, boneless chicken breasts
finely grated rind and juice of 2 limes
30ml/2 tbsp sugar
10ml/2 tsp dried oregano
2.5ml/½ tsp cayenne pepper
5ml/1 tsp ground cinnamon
2 onions
3 (bell) peppers (1 red, 1 yellow or
    orange and 1 green)
45ml/3 tbsp vegetable oil
guacamole, salsa and sour cream,
    to serve

For the tortillas

250g/9oz/2¼ cups plain (all-
    purpose) flour, sifted
1.5ml/¼ tsp baking powder
pinch of salt
50g/2oz/¼ cup lard
60ml/4 tbsp warm water

Fajitas are flour tortillas which are brought to the table freshly cooked. Guests add their own fillings before folding the tortillas and tucking in.

Burritos with Chicken and Rice

Serves 4

90g/3½ oz/½ cup long grain rice
15ml/1 tbsp vegetable oil
1 onion, chopped
2.5ml/½ tsp ground cloves
5ml/1 tsp dried, or fresh oregano
200g/7oz can chopped tomatoes in
    tomato juice
2 skinless, boneless chicken breasts
150g/5oz/1¼ cups grated Monterey
    Jack or mild Cheddar cheese
60ml/4 tbsp sour cream (optional)
8 x 20–25cm/8–10in fresh wheat
    flour tortillas
salt
fresh oregano, to garnish (optional)

1 Bring a pan of lightly salted water to the boil. Add the rice and cook for 8 minutes. Drain, rinse and then drain again.

2 Heat the oil in a large pan. Add the onion, with the ground cloves and oregano, and fry for 2–3 minutes. Stir in the rice and tomatoes and cook over a low heat until all the tomato juice has been absorbed. Set the pan aside.

3 Put the chicken breasts in a large pan, pour in enough water to cover and bring to the boil. Lower the heat and simmer for about 10 minutes or until the chicken is cooked through. Lift the chicken out of the pan, put on a plate and cool slightly.

4 Preheat the oven to 160°C/325°F/Gas 3. Shred the chicken by pulling the flesh apart with two forks, then add the chicken to the rice mixture, with the grated cheese. Stir in the sour cream, if using.

5 Wrap the tortillas in foil and place them on a plate. Stand the plate over boiling water for about 5 minutes. Alternatively, wrap in microwave-safe film and heat in a microwave on full power for 1 minute.

6 Spoon one-eighth of the filling into the centre of a tortilla and fold in both sides. Fold the bottom up and the top down to form a parcel. Secure with a cocktail stick (toothpick).

7 Put the filled burrito in a shallow dish or casserole, cover with foil and keep warm in the oven while you make seven more. Remove the cocktail sticks before serving, sprinkled with fresh oregano.

In Mexico, burritos are a popular street food, eaten on the hoof. The secret of a successful burrito is to have all the filling neatly packaged inside the tortilla for easy eating, so these snacks are seldom served with a pour-over sauce.

Tamales filled with Spiced Pork

1 Put the pork cubes in a large pan. Pour over water to cover. Bring to the boil, lower the heat and simmer for 40 minutes.

2 Meanwhile, heat the chicken stock in a separate pan. Put the masa harina in a large bowl and add the hot stock, a little at a time, to make a stiff dough.

3 Put the lard in another bowl and beat with an electric whisk until light and fluffy. Continue to beat the lard, gradually adding the masa dough. When all of it has been added and the mixture is light and spreadable, beat in the salt. Cover closely with clear film (plastic wrap).

4 Soak the corn husks in boiling water for 30 minutes. Soak the seeded chillies separately in hot water for the same time. Drain the pork, reserving 105ml/7 tbsp of the cooking liquid, and chop the meat finely.

5 Heat the oil and fry the onion and garlic for 2–3 minutes. Drain the chillies, chop finely, and add them to the pan. Put the allspice berries and bay leaves in a mortar, grind them with a pestle, then work in the ground cumin. Add to the onion mixture and stir well. Cook for 2–3 minutes more. Add the chopped pork and reserved cooking liquid and continue cooking over a moderate heat until all the liquid is absorbed.

6 Drain the corn husks and pat them dry. Place one large corn husk on a board. Spoon about one-twelfth of the masa mixture on to the centre of the husk wrapping and spread it almost to the sides.

7 Place a spoonful of the meat mixture on top of the masa. Fold the two long sides of the corn husk over the filling, then bring up each of the two shorter sides in turn, to make a neat parcel. Tie with string or strips of the corn husk.

8 Place the tamales in a steamer basket over a pan of simmering water and steam for 1 hour. To test if the tamales are ready, unwrap one. The filling should peel away from the husk cleanly. Pile the tamales on a plate, leave to stand for 10 minutes, then serve with lime wedges.

Serves 6

500g/1¼ lb lean pork, cut into
    5cm/2in cubes
750ml/1¼ pints/3 cups chicken
    stock
600g/1lb 6oz/4½ cups masa harina
450g/1lb/2 cups lard, softened
30ml/2 tbsp salt
12 large or 24 small dried corn husks
2 ancho chillies, seeded
15ml/1 tbsp vegetable oil
½ onion, finely chopped
2–3 garlic cloves, crushed
2.5ml/½ tsp allspice berries
2 dried bay leaves
2.5ml/½ tsp ground cumin
lime wedges

These tamales are among the most ancient of Mexican foods. At one time the neat little corn husk parcels filled with savoury or sweet masa dough were cooked in the ashes of a wood fire. Today they are more likely to be steamed, but it is still a thrill to unwrap them.

Tacos with Shredded Beef

1 Put the steak in a deep frying pan and pour over water to cover. Bring to the boil, then lower the heat and simmer for 1–1½ hours.

2 Meanwhile, make the tortilla dough. Mix the masa harina and salt in a large mixing bowl. Add the warm water, a little at a time, to make a dough that can be worked into a ball. Knead the dough on a lightly floured surface for 3–4 minutes until smooth, then wrap the dough in clear film (plastic wrap) and leave to rest for 1 hour.

3 Put the meat on a board, let it cool slightly, then shred it, using two forks. Put the meat in a bowl. Divide the tortilla dough into six equal balls.

4 Spread a little masa harina onto a clean, dry surface and roll out the tortilla balls to form 15–2cm/6–8 in round tortillas.

5 Heat a griddle or frying pan until hot. Cook each tortilla for 15–20 seconds on each side, and then for a further 15 seconds on the first side. Keep the tortillas warm and soft by folding them inside a slightly damp dish towel.

6 Add the oregano and cumin to the shredded meat and mix well. Heat the oil in a frying pan and fry the onion and garlic for 3–4 minutes until softened. Add the spiced meat mixture and toss over the heat until heated through.

7 Place some shredded lettuce on a tortilla, top with shredded beef and salsa, fold in half and serve with lime wedges. Garnish with fresh coriander.

Serves 6

450g/1lb rump steak, diced
150g/5oz/1 cup masa harina, plus
   extra for dusting
2.5ml/½ tsp salt
120ml/4fl oz/½ cup warm water
10ml/2 tsp dried oregano
5ml/1 tsp ground cumin
30ml/2 tbsp oil
1 onion, thinly sliced
2 garlic cloves, crushed
fresh coriander (cilantro), to garnish
shredded lettuce, lime wedges and
   Tomato Salsa (page 18), to serve

In Mexico tacos are most often made with soft corn tortillas, which are filled and folded in half. It is unusual to see the crisp shells of corn which are so widely used in Tex-Mex cooking. Tacos are always eaten in the hand.

Beef Enchiladas with Red Sauce

Serves 3–4

500g/1¼ lb rump steak, cut into
   5cm/2in cubes
2 ancho chillies, seeded
2 pasilla chillies, seeded
2 garlic cloves, crushed
10ml/2 tsp dried oregano
2.5ml/½ tsp ground cumin
30ml/2 tbsp vegetable oil
7 fresh corn tortillas
shredded onion and flat-leaved
   parsley to garnish
Mango Salsa (page 22), to serve

1 Put the steak in a deep frying pan and cover with water. Bring to the boil, then lower the heat and simmer for 1–1½ hours, or until very tender.

2 Meanwhile, put the dried chillies in a bowl and pour over the hot water. Leave to soak for 30 minutes, then tip the contents of the bowl into a blender and whizz to a smooth paste.

3 Drain the steak and let it cool, reserving 250ml/8fl oz/1 cup of the cooking liquid. Meanwhile, fry the garlic, oregano and cumin in the oil for 2 minutes.

4 Stir in the chilli paste and the reserved cooking liquid from the beef. Tear one of the tortillas into small pieces and add it to the mixture. Bring to the boil, then lower the heat. Simmer for 10 minutes, stirring occasionally, until the sauce has thickened. Shred the steak, using two forks, and stir it into the sauce, and heat through for a few minutes.

5 Spoon some of the meat mixture on to each tortilla and roll it up to make an enchilada. Keep the enchiladas in a warmed dish until you have rolled them all. Garnish with shreds of onion and fresh flat-leaved parsley and then serve immediately with the mango salsa.

VARIATION

For a richer version place the rolled enchiladas side by side in a gratin dish. Pour over 300ml/½ pint/1¼ cups sour cream and 75g/3oz/¾ cup grated Cheddar cheese. Place under a preheated grill (broiler) for 5 minutes or until the cheese melts and the sauce begins to bubble.

The practice of rollling tortillas around food dates back to Maya times: the people living in the lake region of the Valley of Mexico ate tortillas folded around small fish. Enchiladas are usually made with corn tortillas, although in parts of northern Mexico flour tortillas are sometimes used.

Albondigas

1 Mix the pork and beef in a large bowl. Add the onion, breadcrumbs, oregano, cumin, salt and pepper. Mix with clean hands until all the ingredients are well combined.

2 Stir in the egg, mix well, then roll into 4cm/1½ in balls. Put these on a baking sheet and chill while you prepare the sauce.

3 Soak the dried chilli in hot water to cover for 15 minutes. Heat the oil in a pan and fry the onion and garlic for 3–4 minutes until softened.

4 Drain the chilli, reserving the soaking water, then chop it and add it to the onion mixture. Fry for about 1 minute, then stir in the beef stock, tomatoes, passata and soaking water, with salt and pepper to taste. Bring to the boil, lower the heat and simmer, stirring occasionally, while you cook the meatballs.

5 Heat the oil for frying in a frying pan and fry the meatballs in batches for about 5 minutes, turning them occasionally, until browned.

6 Drain off the oil and transfer all the meatballs to a shallow casserole. Pour over the sauce and simmer for 10 minutes, stirring gently from time to time so that the meatballs are coated but do not disintegrate. Garnish with the oregano and serve. Plain white rice makes a good accompaniment.

COOK'S TIP
Dampen your hands before shaping the meatballs and the mixture will be less likely to stick.

Serves 4
225g/8oz minced (ground) pork
225g/8oz lean minced (ground) beef
1 onion, finely chopped
50g/2oz/1 cup fresh white
    breadcrumbs
5ml/1 tsp dried oregano
2.5ml/½ tsp ground cumin
2.5ml/½ tsp salt
2.5ml/½ tsp ground black pepper
1 egg, beaten
oil, for frying
fresh oregano sprigs, to garnish

For the sauce
1 chipotle chilli, seeded
15ml/1 tbsp vegetable oil
1 onion, finely chopped
2 garlic cloves, crushed
175ml/6fl oz/¾ cup beef stock
400g/14oz can chopped tomatoes
105ml/7 tbsp passata (bottled
    strained tomatoes)
salt and ground black pepper

Don't be daunted by the length of the ingredient list. These meatballs are absolutely delicious and the chipotle chilli gives the sauce a distinctive, slightly smoky flavour.

Ceviche

Serves 6

200g/7oz raw peeled prawns
(shrimp)
200g/7oz shelled scallops
200g/7oz squid, cleaned and cut
into serving pieces
7 limes
3 tomatoes
1 small onion
1 ripe avocado
20ml/4 tbsp chopped fresh oregano,
or 10ml/2 tsp dried
5ml/1 tsp salt
ground black pepper
fresh oregano sprigs, to garnish
crusty bread and lime wedges, to
serve (optional)

1 Spread out the prawns, scallops and squid in a non-metallic bowl. Squeeze 6 of the limes and pour the juice over the mixed seafood to cover it completely. Cover the dish with clear film (plastic wrap) and set aside for 8 hours or overnight.

2 Drain the seafood in a colander to remove the excess lime juice, then pat it dry with kitchen paper. Place the prawns, scallops and squid in a bowl.

3 Cut the tomatoes in half, squeeze out the seeds, then dice the flesh. Cut the onion in half, then slice it thinly. Cut the avocado in half lengthways, remove the stone and peel, then cut the flesh into 1cm/ ½ in dice.

4 Add the tomatoes, onion and avocado to the seafood with the oregano and seasoning. Squeeze the remaining lime and pour over the juice. Garnish with oregano and serve, with crusty bread and lime wedges, if liked.

This famous dish is particularly popular along Mexico's western seaboard, in places such as Acapulco. It consists of very fresh raw fish, "cooked" by the action of lime juice.

Salt Cod for Christmas Eve

1 Put the cod in a bowl and pour over enough cold water to cover. Soak for 24 hours, changing the water at least five times during this period.

2 Drain the cod and remove the skin using a large sharp knife. Shred the flesh finely using two forks, and put it into a bowl. Set it aside.

3 Heat half the oil in a large frying pan. Add the onion slices and fry over a moderate heat until the onion has softened and is translucent.

4 Remove the onion from the pan and set aside. Make sure you transfer the oil with the onion as it is an important flavouring in this dish and mustn't be discarded. In the same pan add the remaining olive oil. When the oil is hot but not smoking, add the crushed garlic and fry gently for 2 minutes.

5 Add the canned tomatoes and their juice to the pan with the garlic. Cook over a medium-high heat for about 20 minutes, stirring occasionally, until the mixture has reduced and thickened.

6 Meanwhile, spread out the slivered almonds in a single layer in a large heavy-based frying pan. Toast them over a moderate heat for a few minutes, shaking the pan lightly throughout the process so that they turn golden brown all over. Do not let them burn.

7 Add the chilli slices and stuffed olives to the toasted almonds.

8 Stir in the shredded fish, mixing it in thoroughly, and cook for 20 minutes more, stirring occasionally, until the mixture is almost dry.

9 Season to taste, add the parsley and cook for a further 2–3 minutes. Garnish with parsley leaves and serve in bowls, with crusty bread.

Serves 6

450g/1lb dried salt cod
105ml/7 tbsp extra virgin olive oil
1 onion, halved and thinly sliced
4 garlic cloves, crushed
2 x 400g/14oz cans chopped
    tomatoes in tomato juice
75g/3oz/¾ cup slivered almonds
75g/3oz/½ cup pickled jalapeño
    chilli slices
115g/4oz/1 cup green olives stuffed
    with pimiento
small bunch of fresh parsley, finely
    chopped
salt and ground black pepper
fresh flat-leaved parsley, to garnish
crusty bread, to serve

This Mexican dish is milder than the similar Spanish dish, Bacaldo a la Vizcaina. It is eaten on Christmas Eve throughout Mexico.

Chargrilled Swordfish with Chilli and Lime Sauce

1 Roast the chillies in a dry griddle pan until the skins blister. Put in a plastic bag and set aside for 20 minutes, then peel off the skins. Cut off the stalks, remove the seeds and slice the flesh.

2 Cut a cross in the base of each tomato. Place them in a heatproof bowl and pour over boiling water to cover. After 3 minutes, lift the tomatoes out on a slotted spoon and plunge them into a bowl of cold water. Drain. The skins will have begun to peel back from the crosses. Remove all the skin from the tomatoes, then cut them in half and squeeze out the seeds. Chop the flesh into 1cm/½ in pieces.

3 Heat 15ml/1 tbsp of the oil in a small pan and add the strips of chilli, with the lime rind and juice. Cook for 2–3 minutes, then stir in the tomatoes. Cook for 10 minutes, stirring the mixture occasionally, until the tomato is pulpy.

4 Brush the swordfish with olive oil and season. Grill (broil) for 3–4 minutes or until just cooked, turning once. Stir the crème fraîche into the sauce, heat it through and pour over the swordfish steaks. Garnish with fresh parsley and serve with chargrilled vegetables.

Serves 4
2 fresh serrano chillies
4 tomatoes
45ml/3 tbsp olive oil
grated rind and juice of 1 lime
4 swordfish steaks
2.5ml/½ tsp salt
2.5ml/½ tsp ground black pepper
175ml/6fl oz/¾ cup crème fraîche
chargrilled vegetables, to serve

Swordfish is a prime candidate for the barbecue, as long as it is not overcooked. It tastes wonderful with a spicy sauce whose fire is tempered with crème fraîche.

Prawns with Almond Sauce

Serves 6

1 ancho or similar dried chilli
30ml/2 tbsp vegetable oil
1 onion, chopped
3 garlic cloves, roughly chopped
8 tomatoes
5ml/1 tsp ground cumin
120ml/4fl oz/½ cup chicken stock
130g/4½ oz/generous 1 cup ground
    almonds
175ml/6fl oz/¾ cup crème fraîche
½ lime
900g/2lb cooked peeled prawns
    (shrimp)
coriander (cilantro) and spring onion
    (scallion) strips, to garnish
rice and warm tortillas, to serve
salt

1 Place the dried chilli in a heatproof bowl and pour over boiling water to cover. Leave to soak for 30 minutes until softened. Drain, remove the stalk, then slit the chilli and scrape out the seeds with a small sharp knife. Chop the flesh roughly and set it aside.

2 Heat the oil in a frying pan and fry the onion and garlic until soft.

3 Cut a cross in the base of each tomato. Place them in a heatproof bowl and pour over boiling water to cover. After 3 minutes, lift the tomatoes out on a slotted spoon and plunge them into a bowl of cold water. Drain. The skins will have begun to peel back.

4 Skin the tomatoes completely, then cut them in half and scoop out the seeds. Chop the flesh into 1cm/½ in cubes and add it to the onion mixture, with the chopped chilli. Stir in the ground cumin and cook for 10 minutes, stirring occasionally.

5 Tip the mixture into a food processor or blender. Add the stock and process on high speed until smooth.

6 Pour the mixture into a large pan, add the ground almonds and stir over a low heat for 2–3 minutes. Stir in the crème fraîche until it has been incorporated completely.

7 Squeeze the juice from the lime half and stir it into the sauce. Season with salt to taste, then slowly increase the heat and bring the sauce to simmering point.

8 Add the prawns and heat for 2–3 minutes, depending on size, until warmed through. Serve on a bed of rice, garnished with fresh coriander and strips of spring onions, and offer warm tortillas separately.

Ground almonds add an interesting texture to the creamy, piquant sauce that accompanies these prawns.

Mushrooms with Chipotle Chillies

Serves 6

2 chipotle chillies
450g/1lb/6 cups button (white)
    mushrooms
60ml/4 tbsp vegetable oil
1 onion, finely chopped
2 garlic cloves, crushed or chopped
salt
small bunch of fresh coriander
    (cilantro), to garnish

1 Soak the dried chillies in a bowl of hot water for about 10 minutes until they are softened. Drain, cut off the stalks, then slit the chillies and scrape out the seeds. Chop the flesh finely.

2 Trim the mushrooms, then clean them with a damp cloth or kitchen paper. If they are large, cut them in half.

3 Heat the oil in a large frying pan. Add the onion, garlic, chillies and mushrooms and stir until evenly coated in the oil. Fry for 6–8 minutes, stirring occasionally, until the onion and mushrooms are tender. Season to taste and spoon into a serving dish. Chop some of the coriander, leaving some whole leaves, and use to garnish. Serve hot.

COOK'S TIP
Baby button (white) mushrooms are perfect for this dish, if you can get them. You can, of course, use any white mushrooms, but larger ones may be better halved or quartered.

Chipotle chillies are jalapeños that have been smoke-dried. Their smoky flavour is the perfect foil for the mushrooms in this vibrant salad.

Green Beans with Eggs

Serves 6

300g/11oz runner (string) beans,
    topped, tailed and halved
30ml/2 tbsp vegetable oil
1 onion, halved and thinly sliced
3 eggs
50g/2oz/½ cup grated Monterey
    Jack or mild Cheddar cheese
strips of lemon rind, to garnish
salt and ground black pepper

This is an unusual way of cooking green beans, but tastes delicious. Try this dish as an accompaniment to a simple roast.

1 Bring a pan of water to the boil, add the beans and cook for 5–6 minutes or until tender. Drain in a colander, rinse under cold water to preserve the bright colour, then drain the beans once more.

2 Heat the oil in a frying pan and fry the onion slices for 3–4 minutes until soft and translucent. Break the eggs into a bowl and beat them with seasoning.

3 Add the egg mixture to the onion. Cook slowly over a moderate heat, stirring constantly so that the egg is lightly scrambled. The egg should be moist throughout. Do not overcook.

4 Add the beans to the pan and cook for a few minutes until warmed through. Tip the mixture into a heated serving dish, sprinkle with the grated cheese and garnish with lemon rind and serve.

VARIATION
Freshly grated Parmesan can be used instead of the Monterey Jack or Cheddar cheese for a sharper flavour.

Potato Cakes

Makes 10

600g/1lb 6oz potatoes
115g/4oz/1 cup grated Cheddar
 cheese
2.5ml/½ tsp salt
50g/2oz/⅓ cup drained pickled
 jalapeño chilli slices, finely
 chopped (optional)
1 egg, beaten
small bunch of fresh coriander
 (cilantro), finely chopped
plain (all-purpose) flour, for shaping
oil, for shallow frying
fresh citrus salsa, to serve

1 Peel the potatoes and halve them if large. Add them to a pan of cold water. Bring to the boil and cook for about 30 minutes, until tender. Drain, return to the pan and mash. The mash should not be smooth.

2 Scrape the potato into a bowl and stir in the grated cheese, with the salt and the chopped jalapeños, if using. Stir in the beaten egg and most of the chopped coriander and mix to a dough.

3 When the dough is cool enough to handle, put it on a board. With floured hands, divide it into ten pieces of equal size. Shape each piece into a ball, then flatten to a cake.

4 Heat the oil in a large frying pan. Fry the potato cakes, in batches if necessary, for 2–3 minutes over a moderate heat. Turn them over and cook until both sides are golden. Pile on a platter, sprinkle with salt and the remaining chopped coriander and serve with salsa.

COOK'S TIP

To make a simple citrus salsa, remove the peel and pith from 2 large oranges and 2 limes and discard. Cut the orange and lime segments from the surrounding membranes and coarsely chop. Gently toss the orange and lime with 5ml/1tsp chopped fresh coriander (cilantro), 5ml/1tsp finely chopped chile, 10ml/2tsp white wine vinegar and 15ml/1tbsp extra-virgin olive oil until thoroughly combined. The salsa can be made ahead and kept in the refrigerator if necessary.

*Quick and easy to make, these potato cakes are
delicious. Serve them with salsa as a light meal, or
as an accompaniment to roast or pan-fried meat.*

Refried Beans

Serves 4

25g/1oz/2 tbsp lard
2 onions, finely chopped
5ml/1 tsp ground cumin
5ml/1 tsp ground coriander
1 quantity *Frijoles de Olla*, see Cook's
    Tip
3 garlic cloves, crushed
small bunch of fresh coriander
    (cilantro)
50g/2oz feta cheese
salt

COOK'S TIP

To make the frijoles de olla, soak
250g/9oz/1½ cups dried pinto
beans in water overnight. Drain
the beans, rinse and drain again.
Put 1.75litres/3 pints/7½ cups
water in a pan, bring to the boil
and add the beans. Cut 2 onions
in half and add to the pan, with 10
peeled garlic cloves. Boil again,
lower the heat and simmer for 1½
hours until the beans are tender
and there is only a little liquid left.

*These are not actually fried
twice, but they are cooked
twice, first as frijoles de olla
and then by frying in lard.*

1 Melt the lard in a large frying pan. Add the onions, cumin and ground
coriander. Cook gently over a low heat for about 30 minutes or until the
onions caramelize and become soft.

2 Add a ladleful of the soft, cooked beans. Fry them for only a few
minutes, simply to heat. Mash the beans into the onions as they cook,
using a fork or a potato masher. Continue until all the beans have been
added, a little at a time, then stir in the crushed garlic.

3 Lower the heat and cook the beans to form a thick paste. Season
with salt and spoon into a warmed serving dish. Chop the fresh coriander
and sprinkle most of them over the beans. Crumble the feta cheese
over the top, then garnish with the reserved coriander.

Chayote Salad

Serves 4

2 chayotes
2 firm tomatoes
1 small onion, finely chopped
finely sliced strips of fresh red and
  green chilli, to garnish

For the dressing

2.5ml/½ tsp Dijon mustard
2.5ml/½ tsp ground anise
90ml/6 tbsp white wine vinegar
60ml/4 tbsp olive oil
salt and ground black pepper

1 Bring a pan of water to the boil. Peel the chayotes, cut them in half and remove the seeds. Add them to the boiling water. Lower the heat and simmer for 20 minutes or until the chayotes are tender. Drain and set them aside to cool.

2 Meanwhile, peel the tomatoes. Cut a cross in the base of each tomato. Place them in a heatproof bowl and pour over boiling water to cover. After 3 minutes, lift the tomatoes out on a slotted spoon and plunge them into a bowl of cold water. Drain. The skins will have begun to peel back from the crosses. Remove the skins completely and cut the tomatoes into wedges.

3 Make the dressing by combining all the ingredients in a screw top jar. Close the lid tightly and shake the jar vigorously.

4 Cut the chayotes into wedges and place in a bowl with the tomato and onion. Pour over the dressing and serve garnished with strips of fresh red and green chilli.

Cool and refreshing, this salad is ideal on its own or with fish or chicken dishes. The soft flesh of the chayotes absorbs the flavour of the dressing beautifully.

Coconut Custard

Serves 6

225g/8oz/1 cup sugar
250ml/8fl oz/1 cup water
1 cinnamon stick, about 7.5cm/3in in
  length
175g/6oz/2 cups desiccated (dry
  unsweetened shredded) coconut
750ml/1¼ pints/3 cups milk
4 eggs
175ml/6fl oz/¾ cup whipping cream
50g/2oz/½ cup chopped almonds,
  toasted
strips of orange rind, to decorate

1 To make the cinnamon syrup, place the sugar and water in a very large pan, add the cinnamon stick and bring to the boil. Lower the heat and simmer, uncovered, for 5 minutes.

2 Add the coconut and cook over a low heat, stirring occasionally, for 5 minutes. Stir in the milk until the mixture has thickened slightly. Remove the cinnamon stick. Remove from the heat.

3 Whisk the eggs until light and fluffy. Gradually incorporate the coconut mixture, then scrape into a clean pan.

4 Cook over a low heat, stirring constantly, until the mixture becomes a thick custard. Cool, then chill. Just before serving, whip the cream. Transfer to individual bowls, top with the cream, chopped almonds and orange rind, and serve. Toasted flaked almonds also go well with this.

VARIATION
Use about 115g/4oz/1 cup fresh coconut, grated, if you can find it.

Light and creamy, this is the perfect pudding for serving after a spicy main course. Children like it, and it is ideal for entertaining as it can be made ahead of time and kept in the refrigerator overnight.

Buñuelos

1 Sift the flour, salt, baking powder and ground anise into a mixing bowl. Add 30ml/2 tbsp of the caster sugar.

2 Place the egg and milk in a small jug or pitcher and whisk well with a fork. Melt the butter in a small pan.

3 Pour the egg mixture and milk gradually into the flour, stirring all the time, until well blended, then add the melted butter. Mix first with a wooden spoon and then with your hands to make a soft dough.

4 Lightly flour a work surface, tip out the dough on to it and knead for about 10 minutes, until smooth.

5 Divide the dough into 12 pieces and roll into balls. Slightly flatten each ball with your hand and then make a hole in the centre with the floured handle of a wooden spoon.

6 Heat the oil for deep frying to a temperature of 190°C/375°F, or until a cube of dried bread, added to the oil, floats and then turns a golden colour in 30–60 seconds. Fry the buñuelos in small batches until they are puffy and golden brown, turning them once or twice during cooking. As soon as they are golden, lift them out of the oil using a slotted spoon and lie them on a double layer of kitchen paper to drain.

7 Mix the remaining caster sugar with the ground cinnamon in a small bowl. Add the buñuelos, one at a time, while they are still warm, toss them in the mixture until they are lightly coated and either serve at once or leave to cool. Decorate with cinnamon sticks.

Makes 12
225g/8oz/2 cups plain (all-purpose) flour
pinch of salt
5ml/1 tsp baking powder
2.5ml/½ tsp ground anise
115g/4oz/½ cup caster (superfine) sugar
1 large egg
120ml/4fl oz/½ cup milk
50g/2oz/¼ cup butter
oil, for deep frying
10ml/2 tsp ground cinnamon
cinnamon sticks, to decorate

These lovely little puffs look like miniature doughnuts and taste so good it is hard not to over-indulge. Make them for brunch, or simply serve them with a cup of cafe con leche or cafe de olla.

Fruit-filled Empanadas

1 Combine the flour and sugar in a mixing bowl. Rub in the chilled cubes of butter until the mixture resembles fine breadcrumbs.

2 Beat the egg yolk and add to the flour mixture. Add iced water to make a smooth dough. Shape it into a ball.

3 Melt the butter for the filling in a pan. Add the plantains, cloves and cinnamon and cook over a moderate heat for 2–3 minutes. Stir in the raisins, with the orange rind and juice. Lower the heat so that the mixture barely simmers. Cook for about 15 minutes, until the raisins are plump and the juice has evaporated. Set the mixture aside to cool.

4 Preheat the oven to 200°C/400°F/Gas 6. Roll out the pastry on a lightly floured surface. Cut it into 10cm/4in rounds. Place the rounds on a baking sheet and spoon on a little of the filling. Dampen the rim of the pastry rounds with water, fold the pastry over the filling and crimp the edges to seal.

5 Brush the empanadas with milk. Bake them, in batches if necessary, for about 15 minutes or until they are golden. Allow to cool a little, sprinkle with caster sugar and serve warm, with whole almonds and orange wedges.

COOK'S TIP
Use a little of the leftover egg white instead of milk for glazing the pastry, if you like.

Makes 12
275g/10oz/2½ cups plain (all-purpose) flour
25g/1oz/2 tbsp caster (superfine) sugar, plus extra for sprinkling
90g/3½ oz/scant ½ cup chilled butter, cubed
1 egg yolk
milk, to glaze
whole almonds and orange wedges, to serve

For the filling
25g/1oz/2 tbsp butter
3 ripe plantains, peeled and mashed
2.5ml/½ tsp ground cloves
5ml/1 tsp ground cinnamon
225g/8oz/1⅓ cups raisins
grated rind and juice of 2 oranges

Imagine biting through crisp buttery pastry to discover a rich fruity filling flavoured with oranges and cinnamon. These are the stuff that dreams are made of.

Drunken Plantain

Serves 6

3 ripe plantains
50g/2oz/¼ cup butter, diced
45ml/3 tbsp rum
grated rind and juice of 1 small
    orange
5ml/1 tsp ground cinnamon
50g/2oz/¼ cup soft dark brown
    sugar
50g/2oz/½ cup whole almonds, in
    their skins
fresh mint sprigs, to decorate
crème fraîche or thick double (heavy)
    cream, to serve

1 Preheat the oven to 180°C/350°F/Gas 4. Peel the plantains and cut them in half lengthways. Put the pieces in a shallow baking dish, dot them all over with butter, then spoon over the rum and orange juice.

2 Mix the orange rind, cinnamon and brown sugar in a bowl. Sprinkle the mixture over the plantains.

3 Bake for 25–30 minutes, until the plantains are soft and the sugar has melted into the rum and orange juice to form a sauce.

4 Meanwhile, slice the almonds and dry fry them in a heavy-based frying pan until the cut sides are golden. Serve the plantains in individual bowls, with some of the sauce spooned over. Sprinkle the almonds on top, decorate with the fresh mint sprigs and offer crème fraîche or thick cream separately.

Mexicans enjoy their native fruits and until their cuisine was influenced by the Spanish and the French, they had no pastries or cakes, preferring to end their meals with fruit, which was abundant. This dessert is quick and easy to prepare, and tastes simply delicious.

Nutritional notes

Tomato Salsa: Energy 122kcal/514kJ; Protein 5.3g; Carbohydrate 21.8g, of which sugars 19.9g; Fat 2.1g, of which saturates 0.4g; Cholesterol 0mg; Calcium 144mg; Fibre 7.9g; Sodium 49mg

Guacamole: Energy 108kcal/445kJ; Protein 1.6g; Carbohydrate 3.1g, of which sugars 2.3g; Fat 9.9g, of which saturates 2.1g; Cholesterol 0mg; Calcium 13mg; Fibre 2.3g; Sodium 8mg

Black Bean Salsa: Energy 109kcal/461kJ; Protein 6.6g; Carbohydrate 14g, of which sugars 1.1g; Fat 3.4g, of which saturates 0.5g; Cholesterol 0mg; Calcium 49mg; Fibre 2.7g; Sodium 9mg

Mango Salsa: Energy 55kcal/234kJ; Protein 1.5g; Carbohydrate 12.2g, of which sugars 11.6g; Fat 0.4g, of which saturates 0.1g; Cholesterol 0mg; Calcium 42mg; Fibre 2.8g; Sodium 7mg

Red Rub: Energy 20kcal/82kJ; Protein 0.8g; Carbohydrate 2.5g, of which sugars 0.5g; Fat 0.8g, of which saturates 0g; Cholesterol 0mg; Calcium 49mg; Fibre 1.7g; Sodium 34mg

Red Salsa; Energy 158kcal/658kJ; Protein 2.1g; Carbohydrate 12.3g, of which sugars 12.3g; Fat 11.5g, of which saturates 1.6g; Cholesterol 0mg; Calcium 30mg; Fibre 0.6g; Sodium 8mg

Chillies Rellenos: Energy 605kcal/2512kJ; Protein 18.5g; Carbohydrate 30.8g, of which sugars 1.9g; Fat 45.4g, of which saturates 27.7g; Cholesterol 159mg; Calcium 385mg; Fibre 1.5g; Sodium 478mg

Quesadillas: Energy 372kcal/1559kJ; Protein 17.2g; Carbohydrate 37.4g, of which sugars 0.8g; Fat 17g, of which saturates 10.9g; Cholesterol 49mg; Calcium 438mg; Fibre 1.5g; Sodium 537mg

Eggs Rancheros: Energy 307kcal/1281kJ; Protein 16.4g; Carbohydrate 17.2g, of which sugars 2.5g; Fat 20g, of which saturates 8.5g; Cholesterol 405mg; Calcium 151mg; Fibre 1.5g; Sodium 229mg

Chicken Fajitas: Energy 485kcal/2044kJ; Protein 26g; Carbohydrate 67.4g, of which sugars 15.3g; Fat 14.2g, of which saturates 3.8g; Cholesterol 60mg; Calcium 118mg; Fibre 4g; Sodium 53mg

Burritos with Chicken and Rice: Energy 626kcal/2634kJ; Protein 37.1g; Carbohydrate 82.4g, of which sugars 3.5g; Fat 17.2g, of which saturates 8.7g; Cholesterol 89mg; Calcium 403mg; Fibre 3.1g; Sodium 601mg

Tamales filled with Spiced Pork: Energy 848kcal/3528kJ; Protein 38.1g; Carbohydrate 74g, of which sugars 0.6g; Fat 43.5g, of which saturates 15.5g; Cholesterol 114mg; Calcium 18mg; Fibre 2.3g; Sodium 94mg

Tacos with Shredded Beef: Energy 202kcal/846kJ; Protein 18.8g; Carbohydrate 14.9g, of which sugars 0.5g; Fat 7.4g, of which saturates 1.7g; Cholesterol 44mg; Calcium 6mg; Fibre 0.7g; Sodium 46mg

Beef Enchiladas with Red Sauce: Energy 460kcal/1939kJ; Protein 38g; Carbohydrate 52.4g, of which sugars 1.1g; Fat 12.3g, of which saturates 3.1g; Cholesterol 84mg; Calcium 108mg; Fibre 2.1g; Sodium 331mg

Albondigas: Energy 420kcal/1759kJ; Protein 29g; Carbohydrate 33.5g, of which sugars 10.3g; Fat 19.9g, of which saturates 6.8g; Cholesterol 119mg; Calcium 88mg; Fibre 3.2g; Sodium 322mg

Ceviche: Energy 147kcal/620kJ; Protein 21.9g; Carbohydrate 4.4g, of which sugars 2.2g; Fat 4.8g, of which saturates 1.1g; Cholesterol 175mg; Calcium 53mg; Fibre 1.2g; Sodium 186mg

Salt Cod for Christmas Eve: Energy 353kcal/1473kJ; Protein 29g; Carbohydrate 6.2g, of which sugars 5.5g; Fat 23.9g, of which saturates 2.8g; Cholesterol 44mg; Calcium 97mg; Fibre 3.6g; Sodium 881mg

Chargrilled Swordfish with Chilli and Lime Sauce: Energy 444kcal/1843kJ; Protein 28.8g; Carbohydrate 4.3g, of which sugars 4.2g; Fat 34.7g, of which saturates 16.2g; Cholesterol 118mg; Calcium 42mg; Fibre 1g; Sodium 215mg

Prawns with Almond Sauce: Energy 236kcal/989kJ; Protein 27.8g; Carbohydrate 5.3g, of which sugars 5.1g; Fat 11.7g, of which saturates 5.2g; Cholesterol 311mg; Calcium 140mg; Fibre 1.5g; Sodium 301mg

Mushrooms with Chipotle Chillies: Energy 69kcal/287kJ; Protein 2.4g; Carbohydrate 1.3g, of which sugars 0.9g; Fat 6.1g, of which saturates 0.8g; Cholesterol 0mg; Calcium 14mg; Fibre 1.2g; Sodium 7mg

Green Beans with Eggs: Energy 126kcal/519kJ; Protein 6.7g; Carbohydrate 2.7g, of which sugars 1.9g; Fat 9.8g, of which saturates 3.3g; Cholesterol 104mg; Calcium 106mg; Fibre 1.4g; Sodium 102mg

Potato Cakes: Energy 137kcal/573kJ; Protein 4.8g; Carbohydrate 12.2g, of which sugars 1.1g; Fat 7.7g, of which saturates 3g; Cholesterol 30mg; Calcium 99mg; Fibre 1g; Sodium 96mg

Refried Beans: Energy 193kcal/806kJ; Protein 10g; Carbohydrate 19g, of which sugars 5g; Fat.9g, of which saturates 4g; Cholesterol 15mg; Calcium 101mg; Fibre 8g; Sodium 189mg

Chayote Salad: Energy 104kcal/430kJ; Protein 1.4g; Carbohydrate 5.3g, of which sugars 4.4g; Fat 8.7g, of which saturates 1.4g; Cholesterol 0mg; Calcium 40mg; Fibre 1.8g; Sodium 24mg

Coconut Custard: Energy 433kcal/1792kJ; Protein 10.2g; Carbohydrate 7.8g, of which sugars 7.8g; Fat 40.5g, of which saturates 29g; Cholesterol 170mg; Calcium 168mg; Fibre 4.6g; Sodium 108mg

Buñuelos: Energy 169kcal/715kJ; Protein 4g; Carbohydrate 34.1g, of which sugars 8.7g; Fat 2.8g, of which saturates 1.4g; Cholesterol 21mg; Calcium 63mg; Fibre 1g; Sodium 24mg

Fruit-filled Empanadas: Energy 276kcal/1161kJ; Protein 4g; Carbohydrate 45.4g, of which sugars 15.7g; Fat 9.9g, of which saturates 5.9g; Cholesterol 40mg; Calcium 59mg; Fibre 1.7g; Sodium 80mg

Drunken Plantain: Energy 240kcal/1006kJ; Protein 2.8g; Carbohydrate 27.5g, of which sugars 15.4g; Fat 12.1g, of which saturates 4.8g; Cholesterol 18mg; Calcium 43mg; Fibre 1.7g; Sodium 55mg

Index